You Can't Control The Soul

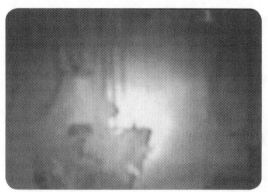

Spirit Entering House

Diana Formisano Willett

BALBOA.
PRESS

A DIVISION OF HAY HOUSE

ISBN: 978-1-4525-0118-5 (sc)
ISBN: 978-1-4525-0119-2 (e)
ISBN: 978-1-4525-0120-8 (hc)

Library of Congress Control Number: 2010917691

Balboa Press books may be ordered through booksellers or by contacting:

Balboa Press
A Division of Hay House
1663 Liberty Drive
Bloomington, IN 47403
www.balboapress.com
1-(877) 407-4847

Balboa Press rev. date: 03/27/12

Contents

Preface

AFTER THE DEATH OF MY husband, Brad, I've witnessed strange occurrences in my home. Apparitions, orbs, and spirits come and go, and they have persuaded me to write this book to convey to everyone that there is life after death and that love continues even after physical death.

This book was written for all those who have an interest in the paranormal and seek to learn what happens to the soul after death. I believe there is a vast audience of millions of people interested in this subject. I have documented evidence of the soul coming back, and the dead do visit their loved ones.

1

Near Drowning

10 years old

IN 1960 AT THE AGE of 10, I was a little girl, living in New York City. My father worked as a stationary engineer in the boiler room of the Bronx Lebanon Hospital. He worked the night shift, 11 p.m. to 7 a.m., so he would be able to be home to take care of me during the day while my mother worked as a file clerk at a company called Joe Lowe Corporation, which made ice pops. It was located in New York but eventually moved to New Jersey. New York was a very vibrant city when I was growing up. I had many friends at school and excellent grades. The school was St. Catherine of Genoa, taught by Our Lady of Mercy nuns.

One day at school, I was outside talking to my girlfriends, and the boys were playing baseball. I got hit by a ball right in the face. My nose started to bleed, and a nun thought my eye was bleeding. She immediately took me inside and washed my face to see if I was all right. The principal, Sister Una, called my father to let him know what happened and that I was going home. Instead, I went to my girlfriend's house, where her mother helped me clean my clothes because they were covered with blood. I called my father from her house; he was worried about me and told me to come right home immediately. When my mother arrived home from work, she called my friend's mother and thanked her for helping me.

My parents were quite strict, and I was to always conduct myself in a proper way in my home. I attended Catholic schools and did very well. After grammar school, I attended St. Catherine's Academy high school. Graduation was at St. Patrick's Cathedral. This is a beautiful church! To celebrate my graduation, we all went to Mama Leone's in downtown New York. The restaurant gave everyone enormous plates of food and, of course, we took half of the food home.

A near-drowning incident took place in August 1960. I was invited to go to a private pool uptown with a bunch of kids. I returned bottles to a local grocery store to get enough money to go, as you had to pay to get into the pool area. One boy, who was about sixteen years old, liked me and told me that if I went to the pool he would watch out for me. I told him I could not swim, and he said, "That's okay. I will put you on my shoulders, and you don't have to go into the water." I said, "Okay," and decided to go with him; my father said it would be fine. We went on the bus to the pool. I put my bathing suit on in the locker room. When I came out, the boy put me on his shoulders and walked around in the pool. All of a sudden, someone pushed him from behind, and I fell to the bottom of the pool. I got up, turned around, and I saw a hand coming down in the water, gesturing for me to take it. I grasp this hand and the hand pulled me up with such force that the water gushed into my face. I closed my eyes and trusted this hand to help me. When the pulling stopped, I found myself at the edge of the pool, safe. I pulled myself up and saw that kid who had brought me to the pool laughing with his friends. I asked him, "Were you the one who pulled me up?" He said, "No. We were all looking for you. Where did you go?" I immediately went home and waited for my mother to arrive. I told her the entire story, and she told my father when he got up for work. The next day, my father went looking for this kid and found him hanging around one of the apartment buildings. My father was very angry and told him, "Did you try to drown my daughter? You stay away from her do you hear me"! The boy never bothered me again.

I witnessed many incidents in our Washington Heights neighborhood. We lived in an old-fashioned apartment house at 9 Fort Washington Avenue; there was a hotel across the street. I used to play outside with my friends after school. Sometimes I saw a black man standing outside the hotel. He was always drunk. At one point, he created a disturbance, and the police were called. They told this man to leave the area, but he refused. All of a sudden, one police officer hit the man over the head with his stick. Blood gushed all over the street. I thought I would faint and ran into my apartment building. What a terrible thing for me to see!

Washington Heights Hotel

One day there was an incident in the lobby. A Spanish man who lived in the building with his family had epilepsy and could not work. I knew him very well. He was standing in the lobby when I came downstairs to play. I said hello to him, but he did not answer me. I wondered what was wrong with him. All of a sudden he fell to the floor; he was having a fit. Another neighbor ran over and put something in his mouth so he would not bite his tongue. That was a day I will never forget.

Once I was trying to sell raffle tickets for the church. I went to the hotel. I was a little scared to go there by myself, but I took the chance. I knocked on one door, and a woman's voice told me to come in. I opened the door and saw a woman sitting next to her dresser. Her legs and feet were extremely swollen, and she kept saying, "Who is it? Who is it?" I was scared and ran out. The woman was blind and disabled. I think she was a diabetic, but I was so scared, I never went into the hotel again.

Another incident almost cost my mother and me our lives. We lived on the second floor. We had an old-fashioned refrigerator that did not work properly. My mother told the landlord about it, but she did not do anything about it. My father worked the night shift, so my mother and I were home alone in the evening. We both went to bed. My mother slept on the pullout couch in the living room, and I slept in a small bedroom down the hall near the front door. I got up in the night, and I smelled something horrible that caused me to start choking. I ran to the couch where my mother was sleeping, but she did not get up. She was fast asleep, and she was snoring. I made her wake up and told her we had to get out of the apartment because there was something wrong. We were both choking, and we smelled a horrible odor coming from the kitchen. The old refrigerator was putting out an ammonia gas smell that was choking us to death. We called the fire department from a neighbor's apartment, and we called my father. The fire department came with a hatchet and broke the front door and the windows, turning the apartment into a terrible mess. I saved my mother's life that night. Thank God, I was there to help her.

I keep thinking about that day I almost drowned. I guess God or an angel saved my life in that pool. My mother said it was a guardian angel. I really believe it was so, based on the experiences I had in my adult life. I continued to live in New York; I went to school and did quite well. When I graduated from high school, I wanted to be a nurse and was accepted by Bronx Community College. I was going to train at Jacobi Hospital in the Bronx; my courses were to be anatomy, physics, nursing, gym, etc. But then I decided not to pursue nursing and switched to business instead. My father was very angry, but he got over it. I got a bachelor's in business administration from Bernard Baruch College in 1974.

While I was school, I obtained several part-time jobs to pay for my college expenses. I worked at Crown Publishing and the Kurt

S. Alder Corporation, which imported Christmas decorations from Italy and Germany. I worked at as a girl Friday for one of the managers at Quantum Science a Computer Consulting Firm. These jobs gave me great experiences.

While I was at Baruch College, my mother found out she had breast cancer. She'd taken a shower and found a lump on her right breast. She fainted in the bathroom when she discovered it. She told my father and me about it, and we made an appointment with our family doctor. He recommended a mammogram, which was done at Columbia Presbyterian Hospital. The next day the hospital called; they wanted to do a biopsy. The biopsy confirmed that she had a cancer. They operated and did a modified radical mastectomy. The cancer did not reach the lymph nodes so she did not need any type of radiation or chemotherapy. We caught it in time. Thank God!

After I graduated, I got a job at Columbia Presbyterian, working for a cardiologist, Dr. J. Thomas Bigger. He was the director of the Cardiac Intensive Care Unit and did a lot of research for the National Institute of Health. I helped him with his daily work chores and to apply for government grants. I met several lovely doctors at Columbia. To this day, I believe it is a great hospital.

Soon after graduation, my mother took me on a trip to Florida. At the airport, I met Julio, a very handsome man from Colombia, South America, who lived in New Jersey. He took my name and address and started to write to me in Spanish, although I could not read Spanish. My mother would go to the travel agency across the street and have these letters interpreted in English without me knowing. The girl at the travel agency asked, "Who is your daughter? Given the things this man is saying about her, she must be beautiful!" When I got home from work the letters were opened and she confessed that she had the woman from the travel agency interpret the letters to her in English. I got really mad at my mother for opening my letters. I called Julio at his home in New Jersey. Another man answered and told me Julio was in Colombia. After that call, I got a terrible letter from Julio. He said he could not continue writing to me and wished me the best of luck. I was so upset; I cried and cried over him. I decided to take a cruise to see if I could find another man.

I decided to go on a singles cruise on the Holland America's line. I got my ticket, and my mother took me to the pier. She saw the people going on the ship and said, "Diana, I don't see any young guys on this cruise. The only people I see are with their families. I hope you can fine some nice guy." I went on the ship and to my cabin, which was an inside cabin. I did not have enough experience to request a comfortable cabin, and believe me, this was not one of them. It was very small, and the bathroom was ridiculous. I could hardly fit in the shower, and when the ship went fast, I couldn't even hold on to take a shower. Wow! What a cabin. I'd paid a travel agency quite a lot of money for the tiny room, which was in the back of the ship. When I told Brad, my future husband, about the price I'd paid, he said I'd been taken. He'd paid almost half what I did, but his cabin was for two people and had an ocean view.

The singles on the ship were introduced at a cocktail party. One woman, Lillian, had two friends—Brad and his girlfriend, Marie. Brad and Marie would come over to the other dining room on the ship after dinner and talk to Lillian, and that is where I met Brad, my future husband. I got extremely seasick on the cruise ship and went to the medical office to get some Dramamine. I took the pills and slept all day. Brad knocked on my door the evening before our last day on the ship. I was so tired, I could not get up. The next day, at my home, I was taking a nap, and my mother woke me up to say someone named Brad was on the phone. I asked Brad, "How did you get my number?" He said he had ways of getting my number. I thought he had to be very smart.

We went to an Italian restaurant in New York City called Orsini's. There we saw Liza Minnelli and the designer Halston sitting at a table with a famous Russian male ballet dancer. Everything on the menu was à la carte. The meal was quite expensive, but it was well worth it. It was November 1977. I met Brad's whole family in Connecticut: his mother, Kay; his sister, Dawn; and his brother-in law, Jim. His mother had divorced Brad's father when her kids were young. Brad had it hard growing up. His mother kept moving from city to city; at one point, they had to eat pretzels for breakfast in the park until his mother found a job. His sister Dawn stayed with her grandmother in Connecticut.

I also meet his aunts, uncles, and children, Melissa and Kristin, who lived with their mother in West Haven. Brad told me he'd got a divorce because his ex-wife had an affair with his business partner. It was very hard for him to leave his home and lose his business because of the terrible divorce situation. He'd recorded the conversations his wife had with her boyfriend when Brad was working, verifying the affair. Brad was able to do this because he was an electronics expert; he even worked at Channel 8 in New

Haven and trained to be a cameraman in New York. Later, I told him, "You should have stayed in this field and not bought your uncle's store." What a mistake that was!

So Brad got his divorce and moved into an apartment in West Haven. By the time I met him, he'd been divorced for about four years. He had a nice apartment, and I loved to take the Greyhound bus to visit him on weekends. I loved seeing Malley's Department Store and Macy's stores as the bus drove into the New Haven terminal. Brad also picked me up from New York when he could, but that was quite a drive on Friday nights.

Everything was going so right, until one day my mother called me at work and told me my father was in the hospital. He'd been taken to the emergency room at Columbia Presbyterian Hospital. My mother told me, "Your father was vomiting and could not stop, and he was getting weaker and weaker." So she called an ambulance to take him to the hospital. He was having a gallbladder attack and was vomiting bile in the emergency room. When my mother told me this, I almost fainted in the hallway of the hospital. I started to see all black, and I had to get a hold of myself before I fainted on the floor. They admitted my father, and my mother and I went to see him in his hospital room. Before we left for the night, my father asked me to bring his watch in the morning when I got to work. I told him okay, and my mother and I went downstairs to have a bite to eat at the cafeteria and then went home. This was around 7 p.m. We went home and went to bed. At 3 a.m. the phone rang. My mother answered, and the hospital told her, "Come to the hospital immediately, as your husband is dying!" He was vomiting, had torn his esophagus, and was hemorrhaging. An artery in the stomach burst because of the vomiting, and he had a heart attack because of the blood loss. He went into coma and died the next day, Friday, January 13, 1978. Friday the thirteenth! We had to contact my brother and the rest of the family. At the time, Brad was recovering from a terrible respiratory illness. He'd had a fever for about two weeks, but he came to the funeral even though he was still weak. This was during the blizzard of 1978. What a snow storm that was. I could hardly walk the city streets. The snow was so high, I would get so tired lifting my feet to try and walk.

Things started to get back to normal again. I got engaged and tried to plan my wedding, even though my father had died. I told my mother that she could live with us and not to worry about anything; she would not be alone. My mother could not get over my father's death. She missed him so terribly much and became deeply depressed over his death. They had been married forty-three years. There was no way I could console her. One day she went to the hospital for a checkup, and she saw the resident who had been in the intensive care unit (ICU) when my father died. He said, "Your husband was calling your name—Lou, Lou—before he went into the coma." My mother called me at work and told me what he said. I told her not to keep talking about it because it would make her really sick. But she kept talking about his death. "Why did he die?" she asked me over and over again.

I took her to see a psychiatrist at the hospital to be treated for depression. Her blood pressure was sky high, 180/110, and I was very concerned about her. I told Brad the next weekend would be the last time I'd leave her alone and stay in Connecticut. Brad understood. That weekend, I was in Connecticut and called my mother in the morning to see how she was. There was no answer at 8 a.m. I thought she might have gone to the store. I kept calling and calling all day. There was no answer at the apartment. Around 4 p.m., I told Brad, "Something is wrong; let's go to New York immediately." We got into the car, and we said nothing to each other until we got to New York. I think we both knew something was very wrong. We went inside, and I called my mother—"Ma, Ma! Where are you?" I looked all over the apartment; then I got to the bedroom. The cat, Snowball, was jumping up and down on the bed, trying to wake my mother up. She was in the bed, dead. I pulled the covers away from her body, and I saw her hand covering her face. It was black. It looked like she'd been burned, but this was dead skin due to a lack of circulation. Her legs had visible clots in them.

I started screaming and called my brother and then 911. My mother had died in her sleep, apparently after a heart attack. Her father and brother died the same way. Her biological mother died during childbirth when my mother was three years old. Then my mother's father, Anthony, married a Jewish woman named Bertha. My biological grandmother had been beautiful. She was tall and had beautiful black hair. She was from Naples, Italy, as was the rest of my family. My father was born in Italy; his real name was Ciro, but he called himself Frank. His sister Angelina was a entertainer in Reno, Nevada. She was a singer and lives now in Arizona with another sister, Agnes. They are in their eighties and still going strong.

My mother wanted to be cremated and not have her body buried in the ground. We honored her wishes and buried her ashes with my father at Mt. Carmel Cemetery in New Jersey. Brad and I started to clean out the apartment in New York, and I moved into his apartment in Connecticut and planned my wedding. We used to come home at 2 a.m. in the morning, dead tired, after being at the New York apartment. We had to sell books, furniture, and other items to move out. It was an extremely exhausting experience. Finally, I left New York, and I settled in a nice apartment with Brad on Derby Avenue in West Haven. It was beautiful, with a nice deck and two bathrooms.

We got married on June 9, 1978. Brad and I had a wonderful honeymoon. We drove to Miami and went on the Royal Caribbean line for a two-week cruise. We went to Venezuela, Haiti, Curacao, Saint Thomas, and Puerto Rico. We had a wonderful time on this cruise, and then drove home from Miami. When we got home, I started looking for a job. I had to leave Columbia Presbyertian Hospital since it was in New York City and I moved to West Haven, CT. I found one at Yale University, where I became an administrative assistant for the Department of Radiology. My husband was still working in West Haven, trying to kept the business going, which was difficult because he had to take out a Small Business Administration (SBA) loan, and he had high payments. The business was failing, and he had to close it down. Brad's ex-wife got married again, and he received $10,000 from the sale of his former house. We decided to buy a home in East Haven, Connecticut, since I was now pregnant. My pregnancy progressed without any problems, until one night we decided to have a nice Italian dinner at a local restaurant, and I drank a glass of wine. We went from the restaurant to Sears to buy some hardware items. While we were in Sears, I fainted on the floor. I was semi-conscious, and the store manager wanted to call an ambulance but they put my feet up on the paint cans, and I started to recover. I told them I was okay, and I was pregnant. I wanted to go home. I got home and had a terrible headache due to the fainting. The next day I called my doctor, and explained to him what happened to me after I drank the wine and he said I would be okay. Even so, I did not go to work that day; I decided to rest at home.

My son, Brad Benton, was born at Yale-New Haven Hospital on June 11, 1979. He was seven pounds and seven ounces, and he was a very beautiful baby. I decided to stay at home and take care of him since childcare was extremely expensive and I was not earning a lot of money at Yale University. Months turned into years, and we had our son tested for pre-kindergarten in the East Haven school system. We were advised to take him to the Yale Child Study Center, where we found out he had pervasive developmental disorder. Pervasive developmental disorder is a group of developmental conditions that involve delayed or impaired communication and social skills, behaviors and cognitive skills. Autism is best known of the pervasive development disorders, the disorders also are known as autism spectrum disorders (ASD's). At the age of four, he was put in the Elizabeth Ives School for Special Children, where he got the help he needed. This school taught kids with autism and were trained to help with the children's anxiety and fear. He also received therapy at Yale Child Study Center. He did very well at that wonderful school.

My husband sold his business and started working in sales at the J. C. Penney store in Meriden. Connecticut. However, J. C. Penney eventually got rid of its electronics department, replacing it with luggage and clothes, which had a better markup. Brad then landed a nice job at Wayside Furniture in Milford, Connecticut.

A store inside Wayside sold appliances, and he worked for the owner. Brad did very well there and made a lot of money, so I just worked part-time at Yale-New Haven Hospital as a medical transcriptionist for the radiology department. I worked at Yale since my son was 3 years old. (In fact, I have worked at Yale since 1982, and now I work there full-time.

My husband was laid off from Wayside after the owner lost his business because of bad investments. I got Brad a job at Yale-New Haven Hospital, where he worked for three-and-a-half years until he became disabled. He had chronic obstructive pulmonary disease (COPD). He had smoked all his adult life, which was the likely cause of his terrible lung disease. Yale took a CT scan of his chest, and there were numerous lesions in his lungs. At first the doctors thought it was a neoplasm, which is cancer. They could not give him a bronchostomy because they were afraid his lungs would collapse, and they would not be able to inflate them again. They put him on steroids, which attacked the lesions. He was also on oxygen at home, but he continued to smoke and developed respiratory failure right at Thanksgiving. The emergency room doctor told me he had to go on a respirator immediately, but Brad refused. They took him to the ICU and gave him an oxygen mask, but he still refused to go on a respirator.

I was at home on Thanksgiving Day, when I got a call from the hospital: I was to go to the hospital immediately. I went to the ICU and saw Brad sitting up, gasping for breath. The doctor told me that he could stop breathing at any moment. I said, "Brad, if you don't go on the respirator right now you will die!" He agreed, and the respirator saved his life. While he was in the ICU, his colon became extremely dilated. The doctors took a CT of his abdomen and pelvis and found out that he had a perforated colon. They had to do emergency surgery, but first, that night, they gave him a colostomy. They cleaned out his colon on a surgical table in the operating room and made sure there were no feces in the colon when they put it back. That night, I was sure he would die. I went home and waited for the hospital to call. I woke up at 8 a.m. the next day and received no calls. I immediately called the ICU, and they were so happy: "Come down right away. He is okay!" When I got there, he was in a deep sleep but he was doing okay. They told me if he did not wake up soon, they would do a CT scan of his brain to make sure he did not get a stroke during the operation.

After the surgery, the doctors told me that while Brad was on the table, his blood pressure dropped to 60/40 and the anesthesiologist told the surgeons, "Stop! No more!" They had to staple his incision and finish the operation immediately. They took him back to the ICU, and the nurses saved his life that night. This was told to me by the trauma surgeon. The nurses in the Medical Intensive Care Unit took excellent care of my husband thus enabling him to survive the night. Brad survived the surgery and eventually went to Gaylord Hospital for the rehabilitation of his lungs. When he was recuperating, Brad found out his oxygen saturation was normal and he did not need a respirator or oxygen mask. We were so happy. He wanted to go back to work.

He was fine for about six months, and then all of a sudden, the shortness of breath returned. He had difficulty going up the stairs. He made an appointment with a very prominent lung doctor at Yale, Dr. Richard Matthay, who explained that my husband's lungs were scarred due to years of smoking and pneumonia. Brad had to go back on oxygen, and all his dreams of having a life again and going back to work ended. He became very depressed and continued to drink. His favorite drink was rum and Coke. He stayed home all day, watching television, and he was really depressed because he could not work. The drinking stopped his medications from working, and he got diabetes and congestive heart failure. I took on another job, doing medical transcription at night for Medquist Transcription. Of course, Brad had a Social Security disability check, which helped pay the bills.

Another problem started to arise when I was at work. My son and husband were not getting along very well. My son was mad that my husband was not working and was always at home, drinking liquor. I had to get an apartment for my son and let him live there while I was at work. He came over on weekends when I was home. I drove him back to his apartment on Sunday afternoons after dinner.

One afternoon while I was at work, my husband drove to see his doctor in Branford. My son was at home that day, waiting for Brad to come home. I got a call from my son around 3:30 p.m., telling me that his daddy had not come home yet. "Where is he?" he asked. He started to get very upset, so I called the doctor's office and learned that he'd left about an hour earlier. I started to worry. Then I got a call from the ER nurse at Yale, who told me, "Your husband is down here in the emergency room." I went down and wanted to know what had happened. My husband told me that as he was leaving the doctor's office, he told the nurse that he felt dizzy. She told him, "You will be okay," and told him to go home, which was very incompetent. Brad was driving home and planned to stop at McDonald's to get lunch for our son and himself, and he forget what happened. He found himself in New Haven, and he stopped at a church. The police came over and asked, "Are you okay?" He did not remember my name or his own. The police called the paramedics, who discovered that his blood sugar was low. They gave him medication to raise his blood-sugar level and took him to Yale. The ER doctors believed it would be okay if he went home. They believed his blood-sugar level dropped because he hadn't eaten anything. We got the car from the church in New Haven, and I drove home.

That night, we ate dinner. Brad seemed okay, and he went to sleep. He slept with a BiPAP machine, and I know the sound of the machine when it works properly. All of a sudden, I woke up and heard the machine making a strange noise. It was 3 a.m. in the morning. I put the light on and tried to wake Brad up. He did not respond. I checked his oxygen, and it was okay. I tried to pull him up, and he was like a dead weight. I finally woke him up, but he was semiconscious. He said, "I am not going to survive." I called 911 immediately, and by the time they came, water was pouring out of his mouth. I took a tissue and tried to stop the water from dripping all over his pajama top. The EMTs told me he has water in his lungs. They thought he'd had a heart attack, but I didn't think so. His blood-sugar level had dropped again; if I had not been there or had not woken up, he would have died in his sleep. They took him to Yale, where he stayed until the next day.

The week before this happened I had not been home. I'd taken my son on a cruise. If this incident had happened one week earlier, we would have come home from the cruise and found my husband dead. I was so happy that I saved my husband's life, but I did not go on any more long vacations because I was afraid something would happen to my husband while I was away. I was always home to watch him.

From 1996 until his death in 2005, Brad stayed at home, just sitting in front of a TV set. Years went by, and I continued to work two jobs. I worked at Yale, worked overtime hours when they gave them out, and also worked as a home transcriptionist typing radiology reports. Between Brad's Social Security disability check and my jobs, we were able to make it.

On January 28, 2005, he went into the hospital because of his gout. His thumb and hand were very red and swollen, and we wanted to make sure he did not develop cellulitis. He was treated for gout in the hospital and released one week later. He returned home and died on February 7, 2005. He was alone that day and was pronounced dead at 5:30 p.m.

That last week he had a visiting nurse. My son was also there, helping my husband. The doorbell rang; the oxygen guy was there to delivery his oxygen. Brad got up to let him in but fell down near the door. The oxygen man told the nurse to call 911, but she said, "Oh, he will be okay," and left. My son wanted to call 911, but my husband refused and told him not to tell me anything about this incident. I decided to stay home and watch my husband Friday, Saturday, and Sunday. My son returned to his apartment on Saturday, and I told my husband, "Let's go back to the hospital on Sunday," as the gout was returning, and his thumb and hand were extremely red. He did not want to go and wanted to wait for the nurse, Jennifer, to return on Monday and check him out. I got mad and told him, "Let's go back to the hospital before Monday when I have to go back to work." He refused and wanted me to go to work on Monday. I said, "Okay, but I told my husband that I will call him in the morning."

That Monday, I went to work and called Brad at noon. He told me Jennifer had left, and she did not think it was for him to go back to the hospital to be treated for gout. She said that Dr. Lam, his primary-care physician, could treat him. I disagreed and told Brad, "As soon as I come home tonight we are going to the hospital." I called him again around 3:30 p.m. and asked Brad how he was doing. He told me, "No good. Something is happening to me. I can't go downstairs and change my colostomy bag. I feel weak. I immediately told him to cancel the oxygen delivery for 4 p.m. and wait until I got home. I told him to cancel the delivery because I felt he was too weak to get up and open the door for the oxygen men to come in from the family room and deliver the oxygen.

I called him again at 5:30 p.m., and a police officer answered the phone. I asked, "Where is my husband," and he said, "The paramedics are working on him." I wanted to talk to them, but the officer told me to come home right away. I finally got a cab, and by the time I arrived at the house, there were two East Haven police officers waiting for me at the door. They told me, "I am so sorry!" My husband lay dead on the floor, covered with a sheet. They had a lot of nerve leaving my husband there and allowing me to see that terrible sight. I started screaming. I pulled the sheet back and saw my husband with part of an endotracheal tube in his mouth. His arm was extended and a bandage was on it; they must have put in an IV.

My son knew nothing about this. He called me when I got home, but I did not tell him his father had died. I told him,

"Daddy went to the hospital, and I will pick you up and take you over the house." I had to wait until the undertaker picked my husband's body up. I left to pick my son up at his apartment. He came in and asked me, "Why is the dining room table moved?" I told him, "The paramedics had to move the table to work on your father. Your father died." My son was crying and crying; it was such a terrible thing for both of us. We never thought he would die like this. We had the wake at Clancy's Funeral Home in East Haven, and he was buried at All Saints Cemetery in North Haven. It was a terribly cold day. We went home after the funeral, and I ordered some food from a local restaurant for our guests. I stayed home for one week after the funeral, and my son and I rested as much as we could, trying to adjust to my husband's death. Brad left a substantial insurance policy, which really helped us out during that stressful time.

2

Paranormal Activity

Orb entering house

THAT FIRST WEEK, I TRIED to adjust to Brad's death, the fact that I would never see him again, and the feelings of unhappiness and loneliness. One night, I was lying in my bed, looking up at the ceiling. The lights were out. I saw a spirit's face looking down at me. At first, the face appeared by the light fixture over my bed. I just kept looking at it, and I will explain what I saw. This spirit's face was distorted. I could see the eyes and nose, but the mouth was not fully formed. It looked at where my husband used to sleep next to me. It seemed to be looking for him. (Later, a psychic told me it was Brad's spirit guide looking at him next to me in the bed!) It looked at me and disappeared.

I looked directly at it, and it looked at me but said nothing. The face was white like a ghost. I thought it could be his mother or my mother. That was the start of the paranormal activity in my house. I put a security system and three video cameras in my home for security purposes and to make sure no one broke in while I was at work. My son moved back to his apartment, returning to the house at the weekends.

It was very hard to get over the loss of my husband. One day I was lying down in my bedroom. I heard music resembling chimes coming from the ceiling, and a shadow appeared near the window. I stared in disbelief as I saw this shadow figure walk to the nightstand where I kept a picture of my family on a cruise. The shadow walked to the picture, looked at it, and then just disappeared. In the picture, I was wearing a beautiful blue dress that my husband liked so much. I guess he wanted to see this picture again, and he was allowed to come down from heaven to do so. The music of heaven is beautiful. It sounds like chimes, but I only heard it for a second, as though heaven opened up for a second and let my husband come down to see his favorite picture.

After that, I was really scared. Any noise in the bedroom made me look up from the bed to see if anything had appeared. I had to sleep with a dim light in my bedroom. I woke up one night, and the light was off. I jumped up and went to the light switch near the door. All of a sudden, there was a noise, as though something were standing in front of the door. I felt it move over to the left of the room. There was something looking at me. I could not see it, but I felt it move. I touched the entity, and it made a sound as though I'd hurt it or bumped into it when I ran to the door. At that point, I was really frightened. A psychic had told me, "Don't be afraid. You are being protected and watched over." Still this whole paranormal and spirit thing was very scary to me. I just wished it had never happened. The haunting is constant and occurs again and again. It stops for awhile and then starts up again. This has been going on for five years and continues in this haunted house.

I was making dinner one evening in my beautiful new kitchen. I bent down to take something out of my oven. I happened to look to the left, and I saw a ghost coming out of the wall in the living room. It looked like a woman, but as soon as it came out of the wall, it disappeared. My son had told me that he could hear movement in the wall next to his bed. At first, I thought it was a mouse, but I began to think the sounds and the movement could be paranormal activity. I started contacting psychics to find out why this was happening in this house. They all said my husband was leaving the portal to the other side open, and others were coming in with him. I believe this is true.

My son heard sounds when he slept downstairs. He heard sounds like someone was touching objects in his room. Sometimes he heard knocking on his door or talking, as though someone was outside the door. I also experienced something rather odd in November 2009. I'd converted the family room to a bedroom and the garage area to a living room; then I put a bathroom in the garage so my son could have living quarters downstairs. One day, I came out of his bedroom and saw my son's image sitting on the floor, smiling at me; then it disappeared. I told my son, "It seems like these spirits imitate us. They can look like us and sound like us if they want to."

In his living room downstairs, I hooked up the DVD player. I also installed three cameras—one in the living room, one outside the front door, and another outside the garage, facing the driveway. The camera images are recorded by the DVD player. I can put the TV on, and review what has been taped during the day. I wanted to put a camera in my bedroom too, but my son said no, because he thought I would get really scared if I saw what came in my room when I was sleeping. Something did come in my room; I was fully awake and saw it with my own eyes. I fell asleep on the bed, and at 11:30 p.m., I woke up. I was facing my dresser, which has a mirror on top of it. In the mirror, I saw the reflection of a man standing by the door. I turned around and saw this man smiling at me. He looked about forty-five years old; he had gray hair and a very pleasant smile. He looked happy to see me. I started screaming, and I fell to the floor shaking all over. My son ran from this room downstairs and tried to help me. I told him what happened, and he was in shock. I was really scared because I'd never seen anything like this before in my entire life. These spirits were now actually coming into my room, and I could see them. The next night it happened again, but this time it was a little different. I was sitting in bed, fully awake, watching TV. All of a sudden a figure appeared right next to me; he said something, but I could not understand him, and then he disappeared. He was very tall and had a cap on, but he disappeared so fast I could not see anything else. I started screaming, and my son ran up the stairs and tried to calm me down. Now I was terrified!

The next thing I did was to buy a digital recorder. My son went to his apartment during the day because he was afraid to be in that house alone. I would turn on the video recorder and play the recording when I came home at night. At first, I did not hear anything, but I kept listening, and then I heard banging. It sounded like the kitchen cabinet had been opened and then banged close. One day I asked a friend take my Chrysler van to be serviced, and I had the recorder on that day. I came home and I listened again to the recorder. I heard a voice, which said, "They found the van." This was after my friend had returned the van in the early afternoon. It sounded like my husband's voice but not exactly like it. I think it was him, because years ago, in 1995, when my husband was alive and he was not too sick, we had a white van stolen from our driveway. The police found the van and the insurance company had the van cleaned up and repaired. This was quite strange; this voice thought someone took the van and then said, "They found the van."

I believed my husband and others were in this house. I could hear a lot of banging on the recorder. All of a sudden, I'd hear a bang, and then I'd listen again and there was another bang. I wondered what was going on. It was really strange, and I couldn't tell what was being banged. I put the recorder on in my bedroom one night, and when I listened, I heard a man's voice. I could not make out what was being said, but now I knew there was something in my room at night. I could feel the presence of it. They were looking at me sleeping. I told my family about this. They did not want me to leave the recorder or the camera on, because all of this was scaring me to death. I got high blood pressure and had to take medication for it because of the stress in the house and the loss of my husband.

I decided to call another psychic service; this one advertised that they could help you communicate with your angels. I called the number and was told that they would call me back at a good time to talk to a psychic. I told them what night and the time would be good for me: Wednesday evening at 8 p.m. I called the number, and a male psychic came on the line. I told him all the things that had gone on in this house since the death of my husband. While I was talking to him, I heard a funny sound in the office, which is where I was sitting. My husband's desk and chair were in there. I heard something move in the room. I told the psychic, and he asked me to tell him the first name that came to my mind. I told him "Cheryl." He said that was the name of my spirit guide. I did not believe him, told him goodbye, and returned to my bedroom to watch TV.

What happened next was unbelievable! I was lying down in the bed watching a show, and all of a sudden, on the right side of my bed, this figure appeared. It was floating in the air and facing the wall. It wore a purple cloth and had brown hair down to its shoulders. I think it was male. I looked at it, and then it smiled. When this figure smiled, I could see the face, eyes, and forehead. It looked like a figure from medieval times. When I saw this figure and looked at his face I knew this figure knew me very well, It knew all about me, and I communicated with it without talking. Then it disappeared. I think this was my spirit guide. It wanted to help me, to help my soul get better after the loss of my husband.

I came home from work a couple of days later and heard that same sound upstairs in the hallway, as though something there was saying "I'm here to help you." That night I went to bed, and I awoke and found myself in the living room up in the air. I could see the drapes moving back and forth due to some type of wind. I swayed back and forth in the air, calling my husband's name. My voice sounded different, weaker than my human voice. I was calling "Brad, Brad," and swaying back and forth in the air. All of a sudden, I found myself flying through the door to the downstairs area where my son slept. In this dream, although I am not sure it was a dream, I told my son, "Daddy's here." I turned and saw a gray chair; then my husband was sitting in the chair, smiling at me. He looked about thirty years old. I bent down and kissed him twice, and he kissed me too. I woke up in my bed the next morning.

Since then, I have read about astral projection. The soul comes out of the body while we sleep and goes other places. I had never believed this before, but now I certainly do. I had an astral projection, and it continued to happen whenever my soul is upset. I can tell you definitely that the soul holds our emotions and feelings. The soul never dies and continues when the physical body dies. The soul remembers love and loved ones. This is why our loved ones come back to us because the soul does not forget love! Remember: love never dies, and this is true.

My experiences were really beginning to scare me, and I found myself contacting psychics and reading about astral projection. One book was extremely interesting, *Projection of the Astral Body* by Sylvan Muldoon and Hereward Carrington. The authors describe a cord that connects the astral body to the physical body. Once the cord is disconnected from the body, you die. They also talked about swaying of the astral body, which I believe is completely true based on my experience swaying back and forth in the living room. I could feel my body going back and forth, and the wind moving the drapes. This wind was my energy. I was fully conscious and remembered everything very vividly; it was not a dream. I remember my astral body coming back when I was sleeping in my bed. I was facing the pillow, and I woke up feeling something pushing into my back. It felt like an elephant pushing me. It was a heavy powerful thing. I did not know what it was. I got scared and tried to reach for the phone, but could not move. I felt paralyzed and thought someone was trying to kill me. Finally, the pushing stopped, and I could move.

Now I know it was my astral body returning to my physical body, and I woke up while this was going on. Believe me, the soul is quite powerful. This experience made me realize that the soul is your essence. The soul is what makes the person. It is very powerful and very crude. It is not a refined or an educated entity. It is composed of raw emotions. It runs on feelings and emotions, and they are what controls the soul. Your mind does not; your feelings do. I had learned a very important fact, which most people do not know. I have experienced this for myself, and now can tell you all. This is why I have written this book: to tell everyone that we all have a soul, which goes on forever and remembers love.

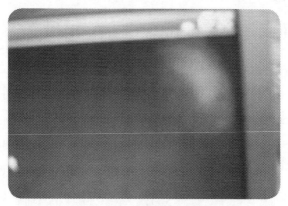

A vortex with face

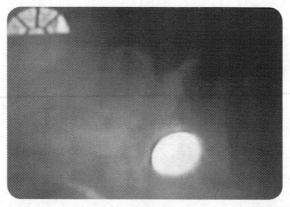

Orb in living room

My son also experienced astral projection. He told me he can see his astral body in the mirror in his bedroom. He said it was all white, with the cord connected just above the eyebrows in the middle of the forehead. He believes that his father got his soul to project out of his body so he could go and see his father in heaven. In my experience, when the soul comes out of the body and goes back, your physical body is healed. Astral projection heals the mind and the body. The mind controls the body. When the mind is healed, the body heals. I know this is true because when I had many of the astral projections soon after my husband died, and I felt really healthy. I go to the doctor every month to get a B-12 shot for anemia, but when I had these astral projections, I felt so good I did not feel tired and felt that I did not need the shot. Of course, I got it anyway, but I could wait another week or so before I had to get that shot. The body gets healed by the soul. The soul goes somewhere and gets healed. I don't know or remember where my soul goes, but when it comes back into the body, it feels great. My son's bipolar tendencies also diminish when he astral projects. This is a marvelous and wonderful thing that God has created. When we die, the astral body comes out of the physical body and goes to the light. Your spirit can come back if it wants to or if it is connected to something on Earth. A loved one, for example, could make the spirit come back. My husband comes back to us almost every day to check on my son and me.

3

Apparitions

Orb with nucleus in it

THEN WE STARTED SEEING APPARITIONS in the house. First, I'd hear someone in the bedroom, near the window, some type of noise as though something was looking at me. I'd decide to go to sleep and ignore the noise. Then, I'd wake up in the middle of the night and see next to my bed the apparition of a young man smiling at me; he handed me something. It looked like a letter, but I could not move. I felt paralyzed. I could see the apparition but could not get up and react to it. I'd try to scream but nothing would come out. Then I'd wake up, scared to death.

I don't know what this ghost wants to give me, but I saw him again after I came back from a cruise. The limo dropped my son and his girlfriend at their apartment, and I returned home alone. I was tired, so I went upstairs to take a nap. I slept for about a hour and woke up to see a man standing at the foot of my bed. He said, "This is for you." He had an envelope in his hand. He looked about forty-five years old and had an accent that sounded British. I got up immediately and was very scared. I told my son what happened, and he was very concerned about me being in the house alone.

I continued to see these apparitions in my room. One night, I woke up and saw a black man sitting on my dresser. He was looking across the room at my husband's dresser, which is where I kept my DVDs. Then this apparition disappeared. It was very strange. Afterward, I received a message saying " God loves the black people," which I now convey to you. This message just came into my mind the next day.

There have been other strange occurrences. I heard someone walking up the stairs from the downstairs bedroom when I knew my son was out of the house. I came home and saw the phone off the hook in my bedroom. My son said he did not do it. I do not have a camera in my bedroom, and I have been thinking I should put one in there. My son and I sometimes have strange dreams. They seem very vivid, almost real. The first dream was the first year Brad died. I woke up, or rather it felt like I was awake, and saw two people standing in front of my bed. One was a pretty woman with long black hair; she looked about thirty-five years old. She was smiling at me but did not say anything. There was a man with her. He was bald but young. He had on a white shirt and black pants. The door to the bedroom was open. The man looked at me and said, "Do you want to come with us?" Then I saw a light in the hall, which turned into my husband.

My husband stood facing the wall and said, "I can't talk to you now. I am busy doing something." I replied, "I told this man I can't go with you. I have a son to take care of." I said to him, "Who determines this anyway?" He said, "God. God does." Then they disappeared, and I woke up in the morning. But these were not dreams; those apparitions were real.

These apparitions have occurred even in the daytime. I went shopping one Saturday afternoon and came home about 3 p.m. I took my new clothes out of the bag, cut the tags off, and put them on hangers downstairs in the living room. I had the TV on and was watching a show at the same time. I looked at the floor in front of me and noticed that the entire surface of the floor had turned black. I looked up and saw a figure standing on the stairs looking toward the window. The figure was all black. It looked like my husband, but the features on the face were different. The nose was small and looked strange. The figure cast a shadow about four feet from the stairs. It looked over to the window and smiled and then disappeared. I think this was a shadow person, which are all black when they appear. I also saw this shadow person in my bedroom wearing a cap and looking at me. I woke up and saw this person who looked like my husband staring at me. I didn't know what these things were or what they represented. I decided to investigate and found out that shadow people are not evil or demonic, but are different forms of spirits of the dead. They choose to display themselves as shadows.

Another shadow appeared a couple of months after my husband died. It was May 2005, and I was writing checks in the dining room. I was sitting in my husband's chair, and I heard movement in the living room. I remember thinking, "Boy, I'm so glad I am going on a cruise so I can get out of this house. This house is really haunted!" All of a sudden, I saw a shadow trying to come over to the chair, but it saw me and hid behind the wall in the kitchen. Then it disappeared.

It was all black but the outline and size looked like my husband. I got so scared I almost fainted. I was so glad to go on that cruise. I did not know that this haunting would follow us on board!

I went to the Department of Motor Vehicles to get my son a new ID for the cruise ship. I already had a passport, but in 2005 you did not need a passport to go to Bermuda; just a birth certificate and ID. We went early in the morning and waited until Motor Vehicles opened. We were there for about one hour, and my son finally got a new ID. We were going on the Celebrity Cruise Lines to Bermuda. We took a limo to Bayonne, New Jersey, where the ship was docked. It was a small ship, but nice. We had to climb quite a few stairs to get up to the ship. We finally got on board and went to our cabin, which was very nice. I got a room with a balcony; my son slept in one bed, and I had the one near the door. The bathroom was small, but we managed. I was just so happy to get out of that house. I was really scared by what was going on almost every night now in that house. I remember feeling really glad that I could sleep in peace in the cabin and not worry about ghosts. Well, was I wrong!

The first night started out all right. My son was in his bed and I was in mine, when we heard someone talk. It sounded like a woman's voice, and she said hello in French: "Bonjour." My son immediately got up. He asked what that was, and I said I don't know. The spirit brushed against my face when she spoke. Now I was getting scared, but I did not want my son to be afraid so I downplayed this. There was a desk in the cabin opposite my bed. We heard movement near the desk. My husband used to like to sit at the desk on a cruise ship and read. I saw his image standing right at the desk. He looked about thirty years old. I saw him for a second, and then he disappeared.

I went to sleep and woke up in some type of daze. I was lying on my back, and I opened my eyes and saw a hand right in front of my face. It took the blankets and covered me up and then waved good-bye to me. I could not move when this happened and felt paralyzed or as if I were in some type of hypnotic state. If you had seen that hand, you would have screamed, but I could not even move. It was a big hand, and when I saw it come over to me and cover me, I thought I was going to have a heart attack. Then it waved bye-bye to me over and over again and left. I told my son what had happened, but he refused to believe me.

While I was lying there, I looked at the wall and saw a light. It was about 3 a.m. Then it just disappeared, and I started having strange dreams. I saw my husband's face, looking at me and laughing. I got really scared and tried to forget about this and enjoy my cruise. Well, things were quiet for awhile. The next day, right before dinner, we went on the deck and took in some nice sea air. My son and I went back into the ship and sat down by the chairs near the window. Behind us was a booth with a woman trying to sell future cruises and shore excursions for the current trip. There was a sign next to her booth. All of a sudden the sign fell to the ground with such a force, it seemed like someone pushed it to the ground. A priest walked by and looked very concerned. After this, nothing else happened on this cruise. We continued to enjoy ourselves and were glad we were out of that house. When the cruise was over and we had to go back, I did not look forward to going home.

4

Spirits and Spirit Guides

A SPIRIT IS THE ESSENCE of a person that takes on a new appearance when the physical body dies. One night, around 3 a.m., my video camera filmed such a spirit entering the house. It entered the house through the front door and went across toward the dining room. I saw this entity fly across the room, a bright light touching the items in my home. I think it was my husband coming back. He was always in the dining room, sitting in his chair and watching TV. We put a TV in the kitchen wall so he could watch TV and do his paperwork and write out checks. This was the area where I saw the shadow; it was trying to get into the dining room and sit in Brad's chair. There must be a reason why my husband kept coming back. I didn't know if he was trying to protect me, tell me something, or just wanted to stay in this house. As time went on, I was determined to know the reason for the haunting.

The camera also recorded a figure in white walking to the coffee table and looking at the magazines on the table. Unfortunately, I can no longer access this footage, and it did not happen again while I had the camera. The spirits know about the camera and will not appear when it is on. I have also learned from these experiences that the soul remembers. This is a very important thing! This is why the soul can come back to see relatives and remembers its loved ones.

I have had numerous arguments with a coworker about heaven and the soul's ability to remember. She told me the dead do not remember. I told her about my experiences, but she does not believe me even after seeing the pictures on my camera. I know, as do numerous people, that the soul does remember. My husband comes back to protect my son and me, and still his love will never die, not even in death. There is also an adjustment period when the body dies. The soul must adjust to the type of death it had and detach itself from familiar people and places on Earth. This period of adjustment varies from soul to soul. Five years after his death, my husband's soul is not as strong in the house as it was one week after his death.

My son told me that he also experienced astral projection. He senses my husband is in his bedroom; when he falls asleep his soul astral projects and goes with my husband. My son told me that his father lives in some type of place that resembles his home here on Earth. He sits in a chair like the one he sat in at home. Things in this house are similar but not completely the same as on Earth. He sees children in his astral projection, and these souls tell him when it's time to go back. He cannot stay. There seems to be some type of healing process as his soul astral projects. He has become more intelligent, and his bipolar disorder has gotten much better. He remembers flying in the clouds with my husband, who watches over our son when I go to work. My son tells me he hears walking up the stairs to my bedroom and someone touching objects there. I have seen an orb entering the house as soon as I leave for work. There is a protection here. There is nothing evil. There is nothing to be afraid of; it is just the love of my husband trying to help me and my son.

The spirits watch over us and protect us, as do our spirit guides. The spirit guides take us on journeys at night to heal our souls. I have been blessed by actually visualizing my spirit guide, a small, unique entity in the air near my bed. It had that brown hair down to the neck area and wore a maroon cloth. When I looked at it, I knew who it was. Spirit guides take on your personality and know everything about you. They love us and try to help us in this life. They also try to heal us when we are so terribly unhappy due to the loss of loved ones. Do not be afraid of your spirit guide for they are here to help us. Embrace the fact that they are here, and they will help you. Trust in them, as the little girl I was trusted the hand that pulled me up from the pool and saved my life. God loves you and wants you to be happy; he gives us these beautiful creatures to help us. Listen to them talking to you in your mind. Remember, they love you and want to help you in your path on this earth.

The spirit of my husband often returns with a familiar smell. When my husband first died, we used to smell his particular odor in the living room and sometimes the bedroom. This odor was of his colostomy bag. He'd had a colostomy after his colon burst and there was an odor when he changed his bag. I don't know why we smelled it when he came back as a spirit; maybe when he was dying he needed to change his bag and could not. I am not sure what it is, but there is a specific reason we smell this particular odor. The spirit is very powerful. It can change appearances, make odors, talk to you in your dreams and also when you are awake. Remember your spiritual being is eternal. When you die, you cast off the physical part that has deteriorated but your essence is eternal.

5

Pillar of Light

Rod of light in living room

I SAW A PILLAR OF light when a neighbor's cat died in January 2009. I'd gotten up a little later than usual because I had a dentist appointment in downtown New Haven. Instead of getting up at 7 a.m., I got up 7:30 a.m., and headed to the bathroom. It was a frigid morning. I pulled up the shade in the bathroom and looked at the frozen water on the pool cover. I noticed something moving around the pool. I looked carefully since I did not have my glasses on and saw the neighbor's cat swimming around the pool cover. I looked at it for about a minute and saw the cat was in distress and could not get out of the top of the pool cover. I called my son and told him to go outside and get a broom handle and use it to pull this cat out. As soon as the cat saw my son, it started to meow as if to say, "Help me, help me." The poor cat was tired and could not grasp the broom handle.

I called the East Haven Police Department and told them, "Come over right away. There is a cat that cannot get off the pool cover." As we were waiting, my son kept trying to get the cat out, but it started to appear fearful and my son got afraid too. So we waited for the police. I returned to the bathroom window but could not see the cat anymore. It had gone under the water, and I was afraid it had drowned. The police came, asked me for a towel, pulled the cat up, and saw it was dead. I was very upset; if I had been up a half-hour earlier, the cat would not have drowned. I was terribly upset and could hardly go to work that day.

I looked at my video camera and saw something strange. There was a light at the top of the driveway. This was before the police came, at the moment the cat drowned. I saw a light with a rod coming out of it, and this rod came down the driveway to the back of the yard where the pool was situated. It looked like something came down and took the cat's soul up to heaven. So now I knew that animals have souls like human beings. This was a shocking thing for me to see, but heaven also loves animals and takes them in when they die. What a beautiful sight this was to see. I will never forget this.

Another morning, I was leaving for work. My son likes to get up early and make sure the house is secure when I leave. On the videotape, you can see me leaving the house and Brad, my son, closing the door and locking it. You can also see a light on the left side of the living room and the rod coming down from the light in the air to the bottom of the floor. On the opposite side of the living room, you can see several orbs appear at the same time. The room turns misty, and it looks like one of the orbs has something inside it, a wormlike object. I took a digital snapshot and put it on my cell phone camera. A face appeared at the same time as the orbs and the pillar of light. I took a photo of the face as well. Those photos appear in this book. I called a psychic and asked her, "What are these orbs and why are they appearing here?" She told me, "These orbs are angels watching over us. They protect us and they are nothing to be afraid of." The two pillars of light are heaven. They come down to protect and to take your soul up to heaven when you die. Do not be afraid, because heaven is a wonderful, beautiful place to enjoy eternity. Do not be afraid when you are dying, because you will see your relatives and loved ones again. There is life after death. I know there is.

I also want to talk about this strange phenomenon called the shadow people. I have been reading up on them and how many people view these creatures. As I mentioned previously, these shadow people are spirits. They can appear as shadows, which require less energy than appearing as a bright orb or ghost. I saw on my camera this bright gigantic orb in the driveway as I left the house for work in the morning. It was 7 a.m., and this orb suddenly appeared in the driveway. It was bright with a greenish-blue hue around it. I saw the orb move to the top of the house and the camera located outside the front door picked it up as it entered the house. All of a sudden the bright orb turned into a black shadow, which moved through the walls and into the house. All the stories on shadow people tend to make them evil, but they are just dead spirits and will not harm you. They will watch you sleeping as my husband watched me. Do not be afraid of them; they look sinister, but they are not.

6

Growing Up in New York City

WHEN I WAS A LITTLE girl growing up in New York, my life was filled with contentment. I was a happy child, and I loved my mother and father very much. My mother was a beautiful woman. She was raised by her stepmother, whose name was Bertha. After my grandfather died, the poor woman had hardly any money to live on, since my grandfather did not pay Social Security. My brother was very attached to her, and when she died, my brother was devastated. I was twelve years old. I remember going to the funeral parlor and viewing her body in the casket. I saw a cut underneath her neck, and I thought that was how she'd died. My mother told me, "Your grandmother died from heart failure, and that cut was what they did when they prepared here for viewing." It was very scary to see. I remember it to this day.

My mother had a brother named Ralph. He was in the navy and was at Pearl Harbor the day of the attack. He lived in New Jersey with his second wife, Chicky. She loved animals. She had a boxer called Dana and birds in a cage. Once, I stayed over their house for a month when I was on summer vacation.

My grandmother Bertha lived on 163rd Street and Amsterdam Avenue. My mother and I went to visit her every Saturday. I used to call her from the courtyard: "Ma-mur." She would open the window and smile as we went up to her apartment. At times the apartment had an odor, since she did not get out a lot, and she was becoming a little senile. One afternoon, I was staying over my grandmother's house for the day while my mother was at work. My grandmother asked me to go to the store around the corner for some milk and bread. As I was returning, I noticed another store next to the grocery store with gypsies inside. They asked me to come into their store, and they looked at me and said what a beautiful girl I was. I got scared and ran back to my grandmother's apartment. Later I went out to play with some friends I met in the neighborhood. I went to their apartment house, about three houses down from my grandmother's. I was there for hours, and when I got back, my mother was waiting outside my grandmother's apartment house. She was very angry. She told me, "Your grandmother was looking for you, and she got upset and told me that she could not find you. Don't ever do that again and leave the apartment area without telling her." I was upset and my mother was angry, but they were only trying to protect me. My grandmother had a mini-stroke about two months after that, and she started to deteriorate. She died of heart failure at the age of sixty-eight.

In 1965, we moved from 9 Fort Washington Avenue to 47 Fort Washington Avenue. I was 15 years old when we moved to 47 Fort Washington Avenue. (We stayed there until I was twenty; the neighborhood had gotten bad, and we found a beautiful apartment at 854 West 181st Street.) I met a Greek man while I was living at 47 Fort Washington Avenue. An H&R block opened up two blocks away, and I went there to have someone do my taxes. He worked there. His name was James Zapantes. My mother had gone there first, and she told me there was a nice guy working there. She wanted me to meet him. I did, and we went out for coffee after work. He seemed like a nice guy and always brought something to the house when he came to pick me up. He lived in a terrible neighborhood called Hell's Kitchen in an apartment house around 48th Street and 8th Avenue. His family had been poor in Greece and moved to the United States and saved a lot of money. His father worked as a chef in a restaurant, and Jimmy sometimes helped his friends by being a short-order cook at their diners. Jimmy helped me when I was going to college by buying me text books. We got along very well. I saw him for four years. I met him when I was nineteen, and at that time I did not want to get married since I was still in school. After two years of dating, I did want to get married and that is where the trouble started. His parents only wanted him to marry a Greek girl. I told him, "This is ridiculous." We broke up when his father died and he and his mother moved back to Greece. My family, especially my brother, did not like him. My brother wanted me to marry someone much better than Jimmy. Eventually, I met Brad on the Rotterdam cruise in 1978. My mother and father liked him very much and blessed the marriage.

New York was a wonderful place when I was growing up. I used to walk with my girlfriend Mildred to 181st Street for a slice of pizza, which was wonderful. We used to walk after school, and one day we walked all the way to Riverdale to see my brother and his wife, Violet.

My brother Frankie had two sons, Robbie and Richie. Robert is now an architect in Detroit, with one son named Michael. Richard has two children, Steven and Kristen, and lives in Minnesota. Richard is a real estate agent and does very well buying and renting homes.

Robert also has an Internet business called Home-Cost.com. He was granted a US Patent for new home construction.

The apartment at 9 Fort Washington Avenue was tiny. As you entered, on the left was my bedroom and next to it was the bathroom. The toilet had the tank on top and a chain that you pulled. Down a hallway was the living room. Next to the living room was the kitchen and next to the kitchen was another bedroom. The kitchen had a dumbwaiter that sent garbage down to the basement. The kitchen was tiny but we managed. I used to sit in the living room and watch television.

One day a bat entered the living room through an opening in the window. I was scared to death, but my father got it out of the house. I sat in a chair in that living room, looking down the hallway, after my grandmother died. Then I thought I saw her in the hallway and that really scared me to death. My mother fell on the floor of the hospital room when my grandmother died. She was very dramatic and made quite a scene at the time.

My mother used to go upstairs to pay the rent. The landlady lived on the sixth floor. One day my mother had gone up to pay the rent and was coming down the stairs. I was standing outside the door, and I guess she looked at me and lost her balance. She fell down the stairs. She yelled at me, but I did not do anything to deserve it. The landlady's name was Mrs. Ryan, and she was always giving people trouble. Once my mother was sitting in the kitchen eating, and some plaster fell down from the ceiling. My mother sued Mrs. Ryan, and because she had a better lawyer than my mother did, we lost the case.

Woolworth's was around the corner. I used to skate down the street and go into that store quite a lot. Next door was a bank. One day I happened to see my uncle standing in the bank doorway; he was down and out at the time and was not working. He was begging for money. I was so mortified, I did not want him to see me. All of a sudden I saw my father walking up the street, on his way home. My father spotted my uncle begging for money. My father had such a look on his face. He ran over and punched my uncle in the face. He told him, "You get out of here right now!" I never saw my father so mad in my entire life. Al, my uncle, was a drug addict, and he was a problem for the family. His first wife, Rose, died of an overdose of drugs in their apartment. This poor woman had to be buried in potter's field. My uncle eventually went to California, went to college, and got off drugs. He joined a rehabilitation program called Synanon. He spoke very highly of this organization, which helps addicts be productive people and get lives again. Unfortunately, Al went back to drugs and eventually died of AIDS.

I used to go to my friend Christina's house after school. Her mother made a delicious breakfast after church on Sunday. We'd go to a cemetery near the school to read the grave stones. One afternoon, we were walking in the cemetery, and I had my new radio my father had given me for my birthday. I was showing Christina the radio when three girls came running over to us. One asked, "Can I see your radio?" They seemed very nice, so I let one of them hold it. Well, all of a sudden, they ran away with the radio. I yelled at them, but they were too quick and left the cemetery. I went home and woke my father up; since he worked at night, he'd been sleeping. I told him what happened, and he immediately got up and got dressed. We walked to the cemetery and looked for those girls, but we could not find them. He wanted to know, "What are you doing in this cemetery anyway?" He told me, "Don't you dare come here again.

Something could happen to you here." So, I learned not to go there again, but only after I lost my radio.

My father eventually bought me a beautiful organ, and I loved to play it. He also got me a beautiful Italian doll when he traveling with the merchant marine. He traveled all around the world. His favorite place was Rio De Janeiro in Brazil; the worst place was India, which he said was very dirty when he was there in the 1940s and early 1950s.

My brother Frankie got married when he was nineteen, and I was only six at the time so I was sort of an only child. My father and mother were very protective of me and made sure I went to Catholic schools—both for my protection and so I would get a good education. I graduated from St. Catherine of Genoa Grammar School in 1963 and was accepted at Cathedral High School, which was taught by the nuns of our Lady of Mercy. There were no boys at that school. I studied very hard and graduated in 1968. The graduation ceremony at St. Patrick's Cathedral.

I got a job with my friend Solange as a key punch operator at Hertz Corporation in downtown New York. I did not tell the supervisor I would be leaving in the fall to go to college. They gave me a test and a physical exam before they decided to hire me. It was a very good company but I left at the end of the summer and went to Bronx Community College, which was part of the City University of New York. I had to pay for my books and expenses but not for my tuition. I got into the nursing program but switched to business, upsetting my parents greatly. They wanted me to marry a doctor and have a good life. Listen to your mother and father because they are always right! They look out for their children and want them to be happy. I should have listened to them. I graduated from Bronx

Community College with an associate's degree in retailing. I decided to get my bachelor's degree as well, so I went to Bernard Baruch College.

While at Baruch, I got a summer job at Quantum Science Corporation a Computer Consulting Company. There was a nice restaurant near my job, so one day I went there for lunch. I sat at the counter and ordered a cheeseburger and fries. The meal was delicious until I opened my wallet; I'd forgotten to take my money with me. I almost fell off the seat at the counter. I did not know what to do. I was so scared and thought I was going to get arrested. I went up to the cashier and explained what happened. I told him where I worked and that I would be back to pay him the following day. He said okay, and the next day I gave him the money. To this day, I never order anything without making sure I have money or a credit card on me.

I graduated with a degree in business administration in 1974 and got a job at Columbia University working for Dr. Thomas Bigger. This doctor was a work-a-holic. When I arrived in the morning, he already had tons of work on my desk waiting for me. I used to go home crying to my mother that the job was not for me. I stayed there because I did not want to travel in the subways and Columbia was close to my home. I did not want to get up one hour earlier to take the subway to work. There were also strange people in the subway, and I did not want to deal with them again. Once when I was in school, I saw a man exposing himself. I jumped right up and, as soon as the door opened, I ran out of that train. I worked for Dr. Bigger until I got engaged to Brad. When my mother died, I could not go back to work, so I resigned and moved to Connecticut.I was too emotionally upset to work at the time. My father died in January and my mother in May which was extremely hard to deal with.

7

Marriage in Connecticut

Our Wedding Day

BRAD AND I WERE MARRIED on June 9, 1978, in Stratford, Connecticut, by Frank Stebbins, a justice of the peace. We could not get married in a Catholic church because Brad was divorced. Instead, we got married and had the reception at in the Garfield Room at Jake's at 6905 Main Street, where Christy Raynor was the banquet manager. We had more than fifty people, and the reception started with one hour of unlimited hors d'oeuvres, including quiche lorraine, tiny meatballs, cocktail franks, barbecued spareribs, assorted cold canapés, and pink shrimp deep fried in ale batter with a sweet and sour dipping sauce. Those hors d'oeuvres were absolutely delicious! The cold hors d'oeuvres consisted of tiny bay shrimp cocktail, melon with prosciutto, celery stuffed with Roquefort, smoked oysters, hearts of artichokes with a delicious vinaigrette dressing. For dinner, guests had two choices: either filet of sole stuffed with shrimp or sliced filet of beef Bordelaise, which came with a stuffed baked potato, the vegetable of the day, and Jake's salad with their house dressing. The meal was fabulous. Then they served a chocolate mousse and coffee, tea, or Sanka. The wedding cake, an Italian cream cake, had been purchased at Marzullo's. The open bar was available for four hours. There was also an international cheese board.

We received a tremendous amount of beautiful gifts and money. My dentist, Dr. Sidney Mondshein, gave us a generous check . My husband's coworkers also gave us some nice checks. We ordered the flowers from Green Leaf Florists in West Haven, Connecticut. Music was provided by the Al De Figg band, based in Wallingford, Connecticut, which did a tremendous job. All in all, it was a wonderful day with one exception: my wonderful mother and father were not there. I missed them very much and was very sad that they could not see their only daughter get married.

The night my mother died I was sleeping in Brad's bedroom in Connecticut. This was before the wedding. Brad was in his home office, doing some work for his business. I had the door closed and the drapes closed. I woke up and in the doorway were two shafts of light that started to move toward me. I got scared and closed my eyes, and when I opened my eyes they were gone. I believe they were my mother and father looking out for me. This was my first exposure to the paranormal and to spirits.

After the wedding, we left for our honeymoon. Brad could not fly because he was acrophobic. One of his assignments in the National Guard had been to go up in a helicopter and take pictures, and this caused him to get acrophobic. He could not go on escalators either. So we drove to Miami to get to the cruise ship, the *Sun Viking* of the Royal Caribbean line.

The cabin was very small, and with all our clothes we had, we could hardly get into the bed and move around. The first week's menu was fine, but the menu was repeated the second week, which I did not appreciate at all. I started to get upset because of the sudden deaths of my mother and father. I was really grieving for them. I felt as if they had been killed, because they were not sick at all; for them to go that fast was a terrible shock to me. It took a number of years to get over their loss. I had been very attached to my mother. I loved and missed her so very much. In Florida, I went to the South of the Border resort gift shop and looked at the gifts they were selling. One in particular really upset me: a plate with "Long life to your mother for there is no other" written on it. I will never forget this phrase. It is absolutely true. All moms should live a long time because when they die the children are devastated. My mother told me before she died, "I love you with such a love." I wished I could have saved her life as I had when I was a child.

The cruise lasted two weeks, and we had a fabulous time. We went to Venezuela, Curacao, Haiti, St. Thomas, Puerto Rico, and St. Martin.

Honeymoon in Haiti

When we got off the ship we had to go through customs. My husband had bought a lot of liquor in St. Thomas because it was cheap there, and I purchased a coral ring with a 14-karat gold setting. I forgot to declare the ring on the customs sheet and was wearing it when we got off the ship. The custom inspector asked, "Where did you get this ring?" I told him "St. Thomas." He said, "You did not declare this on the sheet," and I told him I'd forgotten to do so. Well, the customs officials went nuts! They made me take everything out of my bag. They kept asking me "where did you get this" and "where did you get that." It was ridiculous. We were there for two hours. Brad yelled at me because I forgot to declare the ring. Anyway, they finally let us go home. It was about 100 degrees in Miami, and we just wanted to get out of there.

On the way home, we also went to Disney World, Fort Lauderdale, and Cypress Gardens. Brad's mother, Kay, was upset that we took so long to get back to Connecticut. We started driving home. We finally arrived in Connecticut, and we were driving on a dark rainy highway with highway pillars in the road. I was sitting in the passenger seat; Brad was driving. All of a sudden, I saw my mother's face in the windshield. I told Brad about this, but he did not say anything about it. I felt that my mother was protecting us on this dark, dangerous highway.

We finally got back to our apartment on Derby Avenue in West Haven. It was a nice apartment. As you entered, there was a nice living room and a bathroom on the left. The kitchen was off the living room, and the apartment had a nice patio outside. The upstairs was roomy. We took one bedroom and made an office for Brad out of the other one. There was another bathroom upstairs. We were comfortable there. We put my wedding picture in the living room.

It is a beautiful photograph, taken by a professional named Nino, and I still have it.

I started looking for work after being home for two weeks. At the same time, my husband started to exhibit some strange behavior. He seemed to get mad very easily. When we were cleaning out my parents' apartment in New York, for example, there were a lot of books that we had to sort through and either sell or take back to Connecticut. Brad was sorting through some books when, all of a sudden, he started to throw them across the room. I stopped what I was doing and asked him what was wrong, "Why are you throwing these books?" He stopped, looked mad, and said, "I don't want to do this." I told him, "You don't have to. You can go home, and I will clean out the apartment." He changed his mood, looked happy, got up, and said, "It's okay. Let's go." I found this a little scary, as I'd never seen anyone throw things like that. I put the incident out of my mind and went back to Connecticut with Brad. I thought maybe his outburst was due to the stress of my parents dying and moving me out of the apartment. But he'd also started drinking a lot.

Before my father died, I had stayed over Brad's mother's house for the weekend. Brad came over around 11 a.m. to take me out and asked his mother, "Do you have anything to drink?" She told him, "I have tomato juice and wine in the refrigerator," and he drank the wine. I went home and told my father that Brad had been drinking wine at 11 a.m., and my father told me he would have a talk with him. But my father died and so they never had that talk. I told my mother about this too, and she told me that she did not want me to marry Brad. She wanted me to marry a doctor or lawyer and told me, "Brad is not good enough for you. He will get sick. He smokes and drinks at this young age of 34." My mother and brother were both mad that I was marrying Brad. They told me, "We don't want you to do this." I got mad at them, and then my poor mother died. And I married Brad.

I really did not know him that well. I married him after knowing him for only eight months, which is really not enough time to really get to know someone and their habits. Smoking was another of his addictive habits. He even got some type of pneumonia before we got married, during the blizzard of 1978. He was so sick, I told his mother take him to the emergency room at Yale. He had been sick for over one month without getting better. But she refused to take him, as she thought his family doctor who was treating him for this condition was doing a fine job but it took him two months to recover. When he got a little better we went to a diner, and he took out a cigarette and started smoking. I asked, "What do you think you're doing? You're not smoking after that sickness, are you?" He said, "I feel okay, I'm all right." But it was ridiculous. His body was telling him not to smoke, and yet he continued this terrible habit until he got COPD. We tried to get him to stop numerous times, particularly since every year he developed pneumonia, which led to scar tissue in his lungs. His doctor told me that if Brad did not stop this smoking, he would not be able to work anymore. He did not listen to anyone. His mother told him numerous times. When I tried again to make him stop when he was in his forties, he told me "If you make me stop smoking, I will divorce you." I should have walked out, but I didn't.

Brad also hit our child when he got stressed. Once he hit him on his backside in front of me. The poor kid came over to me and started to cry. I told Brad, "Don't every do that again. His backside is so red." My husband seemed to have such extreme rage. It could have been because of that sales job at Penney's, which was very stressful, but there was no reason to take it out on a child. I didn't know that while I was working at night, he was hitting my son at home. The poor kid was disabled, and my husband would hit him in the face and the head. One night I came home from work, and my son came out of his bedroom. I said, "Hi, honey." He was crying and said, "Daddy hit me." I asked my husband, "Why did you hit little Brad?" And he said "I got mad!" He'd hit my poor son in the ear, and his ear was still hurting. I told my husband, "Never do this again!" My son told his therapist at the Yale Child Study Center, Mr. Stephen Marans, that my husband was hitting him. Mr. Marans called a meeting with me, my husband and the social worker at the Yale Child Study Center who was working with us. Her name was Ms. Cox. My husband refused to go to the meeting since he felt embarrass that Mr. Marans and Ms. Cox knew he was hitting our son. I finally told my husband, "Never do this again, or you will get in serious trouble." Finally, he stopped hitting the kid. To this day, when my son tells me the way my husband used to hit him, it makes me mad, because I did not know anything about it. My husband had told my son, "Don't you dare tell your mother." I told my son, "You should have told me about this, because I would have done something."

My husband's behavior became more and more worrisome. One night he came home from J. C. Penney, and he looked really mad. He had not had his rum and Coke yet, and we got into a little argument about him not making enough money in this job, which paid him a commission but no salary. I was working only part-time, and we could hardly pay the mortgage. I went upstairs after the argument to get ready for bed. All of a sudden, my husband ran up the stairs, opened the door in a rage, and punched me right in the face. He keep punching me, and I said, "Stop! Stop this!" He went downstairs, and I was going to call the police if he ever did it again. But the next day, he told me he was sorry, and I did not notify the police. But I will never forget this. He was like a bully—hitting me that one time and hitting that poor kid. After that, when he got mad, he did not hit anymore, but he either would turn off all the lights or throw the garbage all over the kitchen floor. If my parents had been living, they would have demanded that I get away from him. Brad always stayed in his home office after work, watching TV, smoking, and drinking rum and Coke. He would stay in that room until 3 a.m. or 4 a.m. I'd get up, knock on the door, and ask him, "When are you going to go to bed? You have to get up at 7 a.m. for work. It is crazy to go to bed this late. What are you doing in there?" He'd tell me go to bed, and he would finally get to bed and have to get up four hours later for work. I don't know how anyone could do this and this is probably why he did not have any patience with my son at night, because he was so tired. I eventually told his mother about these strange habits, and she spoke with him about going to bed at a reasonable time. He started to go to bed earlier but would wake up at 4 am so he stopped this routine and returned to his old habits of sleep.

I think he had some type of a mania. Based on these mood swings, I now believe he was bipolar. Both my son and my husband's cousin are bipolar. I think my husband self-medicated himself with alcohol. These things were not known to me before my marriage, as I would not have married him if they were. I did not grow up in this kind of environment. I had a very quite normal home with my parents. They never yelled or screamed at each other, and I was never hit. To hit a small defenseless child who was disabled is horrible. Brad tormented the boy in other ways as well. My son was afraid of the toilet, and my husband made things worse. He told my son, "If you sit on the toilet, you will drown. The water will come up all over the floor." The poor kid went to the bathroom in his pants at my mother-in-law's house because my husband scared him about the toilet.

This strange behavior was due to drinking alcohol, which eventually killed him. This alcohol stopped his heart. He could have lived for a long time if he only stopped those horrible habits. I had to see him in the coffin with black hair; he looked so young. What a shame! His mother lived to be seventy-six years old. She died of pancreatitis. She developed very bad gallstones. One night, after eating spare ribs, she started to vomit and get really dizzy in her apartment. She called her daughter, Dawn, who told her to call 911. She was taken by ambulance to Yale-New Haven Hospital, and they discovered through a CT scan that she had pancreatitis and had developed an abscess. They treated her for the pancreatitis but it did not get better. They operated to remove the diseased part of the pancreas and hoped that would resolve the infection and drain the abscess. It did not work. After the operation she developed sepsis and looked horrible. My husband almost fainted when he saw her in that hospital bed. She looked like a monster, because they had to pump her up with fluid as her blood pressure was so low. Her entire face looked gigantic. She was full of fluid, and my husband went home and cried. Eventually, we met with the surgeon who explained that she could not tolerate another operation. The family decided to turn off the ventilator, and she died.

8

Working in New Haven

AFTER THE HONEYMOON, I LOOKED for a job. I wanted to work for the Connecticut Telephone Company. My sister-in-law was a manager there, and I thought it would be easy to get hired there. Well, that was a mistake! I went down to the telephone company and applied for a job. The application asked, "Do you have any relatives working for the telephone company?" I put her name down: Dawn Willett Maher. The interviewer said to me, "Dawn is your sister-in-law?" and I said, "Yes." Well, I did not get any job there because Dawn's husband, Jim, would not let her give me a recommendation since, as he said, "You don't know what her work ethics are." Boy, is that funny. I have worked at Yale-New Haven Hospital now for twenty-eight years. Dawn and Jim did not even go to my husband's funeral. I won't talk about them again in this book.

I got a job at the Yale University School of Medicine in the Department of Diagnostic Radiology. I worked for two doctors as their administrative assistant. It was a nice job and the benefits were good, but the salary was horrible before they got the union. I had worked there for about three months when one day I started feeling sick. It was a strange feeling as though I was in a daze. I did not get my period and found out I was pregnant. My husband sent me beautiful flowers at work, and we were happy we were going to have a child. We started looking for a home, and we bought the house on Morris Road in East Haven. It needed some work, and we moved in January 1979 and started to fix the house up. Brad painted all the rooms, and his mother helped me clean. We made a beautiful nursery with Raggedy Ann and Andy wall paper. We painted the room yellow, and we got a beautiful crib, which Brad's mother paid for.

My pregnancy proceeded without any more incidents or complications , and I stayed home after being pregnant for 7 months since my ankles were getting swollen and I felt very uncomfortable to continue to work.

Brad Benton Willett was delivered by caesarian section on June 11, 1979. He was a beautiful baby, and when he was born, his hair was bright red. The nurse asked my husband, "Who has red hair in your family," and my husband told her his mother was a redhead. My husband told everyone that the baby had red hair, but the morning after his birth, his hair turned brown. We didn't care because he was healthy and he was a nice-looking baby. He had a tear duct problem, and they gave us some medication to put in his eyes to get rid of the infection. One morning he was crying in his crib, and I picked him up. He could not open his eyes. He was screaming, so I called my husband. He took some cotton wool, and wet it, and put it over his eyes to open them up. The medication had made them sticky, and the baby was okay after that.

My son, Brad, had a nice room with an air conditioner. He slept very well, and I nursed him until his third month. I did not go back to the job at the university because daycare was so expensive, it was not worth it for me to work. So I stayed home until my son was three years old. One day, I started feeling dizzy and not quite myself. I found out that I had a goiter and I needed thyroid medication. I was put on Synthroid and started feeling less tired and much better. I looked for a job at Yale-New Haven Hospital. I got a part-time job working evenings and weekends; my husband took care of my son while I worked. I worked twenty hours with medical benefits, which we needed at the time. I was trained to be a medical transcriptionist; I listened to tapes the radiologist made and transcribed them using a typewriter. I had to learn the medical terminology, which took me about a year.. I was able to work overtime, which really helped us with the bills.

My husband lost his business, Ryan Stationer and the Office Furniture Center, because of the economy. He had to take an SBA loan out in 1978, which made his landlord raise the rent on his store. The overhead became too much to maintain, and the discount stores were taking business away from him. My husband was able to get a sales position at J. C. Penney in Meriden. He started making some good money because microwaves and electronics were the in-things at the time.

We found out that my son had a disability called pervasive developmental disorder, and we sent him to a special school in Hamden called Elizabeth Ives School for Special Students. He also received therapy at the Yale Child Study Center. His therapist was Steven Marans; he is now director there. This school was excellent. The director at the time was Betty Sword, a wonderful person. My son did really well and started talking more and becoming more social. He had a form of autism with high anxiety which was part of the pervasive developmental disorder, and they wanted to put him on a anti-psychotic medication. But I was afraid to give him a medication like that at such an early age because it had tremendous side effects. So, I said, "No, just give him therapy and let him go to school." This helped him tremendously, but we did have some moments. Our house had a window that looked out on the backyard. We planted flowers and tomato plants there. One day, I was looking out the window when I saw my son stepping on the flowers. I did not say anything to him, but I did tell his therapist, and he replied to me, "Brad is a disturbed boy."

We continued with therapy and school, however, and Brad continued to do well. We thought he could go to the middle school in East Haven as long as he was in a special class. Mr. Stephen Marans agreed. At the next school meeting, we put him in with regular kids. Those kids were off the wall. They teased the kid. They wanted the girls to have sex with him. My son was 13 years old at this time. Finally he had a breakdown, and we kept him home from school until the board of education in East Haven agreed to return him to the Ives School. He eventually graduated from there, and we found a wonderful high school for him in Milford, called the Foundation High School. He found a nice girlfriend, and he started work study at the Christmas Tree Shop in Orange. The school was very proud of him and when he left the class, the Christmas Tree Shop hired him because they were very pleased with his work.

What concerned me was what my son told me about my husband and his rages when I was working. My son told me my husband used to hit him for any little thing. He hit him in the head and in the ear. He punched the kid in the face. I was not aware of this because my husband told my son, "Do not tell your mother." One night I came home from work, and my son came out of his bedroom. I said, "Hi, honey, how are you?" He told me, "Daddy hit me." I turned to my husband and said, "Why did you hit this boy?" He said, "I got angry." I told him, "Never hit this boy again." Finally, the Yale

Child Study Center found out about the beatings, because my son told Mr. Marans, who wanted to talk to my husband. I told my husband, "If you every hit this boy again, you will get arrested." My husband's mother used to watch my son on the weekends when my husband and I were working. My husband would pick my son up at his mother's house and then get me. Brad's mother told my husband when the boy acted up, and my husband would hit this poor boy in the face. I never know the extent of this abuse until the Yale Child Study Center told me about it. I told his mother. She just said, "Why don't you just get a divorce?" I guess I should have, but where was I to go? I no longer had a mother or father, and my brother and his family were never around. They hardly ever called. So I was basically alone and afraid.

My husband got laid off from Penney's and got a job at Wayside Furniture in Milford. His boss was Danny, who owned the concession for appliances and home entertainment. My husband was doing great, and my job was secure, so we went on some nice vacations to the Caribbean and Cape Cod. We loved Dennis Port in Cape Cod and went there every summer. We stayed at the Shifting Sands Motel, which was right on the water. Then, Danny lost his business because of some bad investments, and my husband was out of work again. I got him a job at Yale, where he'd worked part-time in 1982, in the film library. He was hired full-time with benefits and a pension, and we were so glad since we could pay the bills and mortgage. He worked there until he became disabled with chronic obstructive pulmonary disease (COPD).

In addition to my job at Yale, I also got a job working at home transcribing radiology reports for different hospitals. My son and husband did not get along at all. My husband used to say some strange things to upset my son. My husband used to tell him as soon as my son went downstairs in the morning to have breakfast that he was going to call the police today. He also told my son that the Martians were in the back yard and they were going to take my son and my husband to another planet. Either one or the other would call 911; that happened at least twice every month.

The police would call an ambulance and they would take my son down to the hospital; finally we found out he was bipolar. Some incompetent doctors gave him an antidepressant, which made him more manic. He was finally admitted to Yale Psychiatric Hospital and got better. My husband's health, however, got worse. He drank rum and Coke all day. He was a diabetic, and drinking all that sugar made his condition much worse. He soon needed insulin. His legs swelled, and he developed the congestive heart failure that eventually killed him.

I was a widow, and my son had no father. Those were very hard times after his death. To see my husband dead on the floor, covered with a sheet, made me really sick. I became depressed after the loss of my husband, particularly since I had no family nearby to help me. My brother and his wife lived in Tucson, Arizona; I visited them and did enjoy that, but there was no support system for me in Connecticut. My son moved in with his girlfriend, and I was alone in the house. I liked the privacy, but then the hauntings began, as verified by the pictures in this book.

9

The Hauntings Continue

THE VISITS FROM THE DEAD continued. We continued hearing footsteps going up the stairs to my bedroom. My son heard them while he was downstairs in his living quarters. He also heard someone flushing the toilet and watched the water level in the bowl change. One night, he felt fingernails on his hand. As he woke up, he saw the nail imprints on his hand. I was very concerned. I told my son to tell me if it happened again, so I could bring a psychic into the house. I believe this happened because my husband used to hit my son when he was a young boy. One time I was watching TV in the bedroom, and my husband was in his office doing paperwork. He had a rum and Coke on the desk. My son knocked the drink over, and my husband started punching him until I ran in and stopped it. So, when my son and I started talking about those old times, I think my husband got mad in death.

One night, I heard a movement among my nail-polish bottles, and then I heard a bang. I thought something had fallen but could not see anything. I learned later that when a spirit leaves a room, it sounds like a explosion. It woke me up, and I really got scared.

Sometimes, I feel as though there is someone in my room, watching me at night. I am afraid of the shadow people and read that if there is a light on, they do not come. So I leave a dim light on in my bedroom every night. Once, I had a very strange and vivid dream. In the dream, I opened my bedroom door and saw the light on in the bathroom, as though someone was in there. All of a sudden the door opened, and my husband walked out, smiling. He did not look at me at first, but he walked out, he stopped and looked at me, as though he wanted me to go with him. I did not. At the same time, I saw a man and woman walk downstairs, laughing. I saw myself turn, and those two people were my husband and a woman. She had brown hair, looked to be about fifty years old, and looked as though she were worried about me. She started to kiss my face over and over again. In the dream, I asked my husband, "Do you have any money?" He opened a wallet, but it had no money in it. Then I woke up.

It seems as though my husband is trying to communicate with me in my dreams. My son also dreams about him; he told me my husband looks mad and he will wake up very scared. I wished all these things would just go away. If you don't go to the light when you die, you remain an earthbound spirit. My husband did not choose to go to the light, and he continues to haunt us. When the last image on the camera was recorded, I saw faces of the dead who haunt the house with my husband. The portal stays open, and others enter as well. This is a very concerning stressful situation in this house.

If I had known about this when my husband first died, I would have sold the house. But I put in a new kitchen and fixed the downstairs. Since I put all that money into the house, I hope that sooner or later these hauntings will stop. I hope my husband will find some type of peace in death and go to the light.

I continue to check my video camera and the recorded images of the house every morning. There has not been much activity since May 2, 2010. On that day, I got up with a very bad stomach pain, which had started the day before. I thought it was diverticulitis, since I had that once before. I'd eaten some potentially irritating food at a restaurant the night before: fried fish and onion rings. I also thought I might have an infection or some type of virus. I stayed in bed all day Saturday and got out of bed in the evening to take a shower. I got out of the tub and felt sick to my stomach. I fell on the floor in the bathroom, but tried to get dressed and dry my hair. I fell on the bed and called my doctor's office. I knew something was not right. The doctor on call said, "If you do not get better by Sunday, go to the emergency room. On Sunday, I still had pain all over my abdomen. I could hardly get up to go to the bathroom and get dressed. I called the East Haven Fire Department and told them I had to go to the emergency room. They came in a few minutes and called an ambulance. The American Medical Response workers were so nice. I got into the ambulance, and one of the AMR workers talked to me and said, "Don't worry, you will be there soon."

At Yale-New Haven Hospital, the doctor in the emergency room examined me and started to push down on my abdomen on the right side. I told her it hurt there, and she was concerned. She ordered a CT scan of my abdomen. I had to drink oral contrast and wait two hours for the exam. I refused the intravenous contrast since I was afraid to be injected with it. They gave me morphine and medicine for nausea. Finally they took me for the CT scan. They did the CT scan and took me back to the emergency room, where I waited for the results. Next to me was a man who was throwing up, and I had to tell the receptionist to move me away since he was making me sick. They found a vacant room and I waited there for the results. Finally the radiologist said that I had appendicitis and could not go home as I need an operation. I called my son and told him what has happened.

I told him, "Don't cry. I will be all right." I knew his girlfriend was there to keep him company.

My doctor called a surgical consultant, and my surgeon was Dr. Christopher McLaughlin, a very good surgeon. I was taken to the operating room at 3 p.m. and saw the team who would be operating on me. I remember them talking to me and then, all of a sudden, I woke up in the recovery room. I didn't remember anything. I woke up just as if I had been taking a nap. I had no side effects at all. They did a laparoscopic appendectomy, and I was able to go home the next day. I did have pain around my abdomen, because they had to pump up my colon with carbon dioxide to operate. I was a little sore, but it was not too bad. stayed home for one week and then went back to work. I felt tired for about two weeks and then felt like myself again. I was really lucky the appendix did not burst; the pathology report said perforation had been possible since the appendix was hemorrhaging. So I was very lucky I went to the hospital when I did.

I spoke to a psychic because the activity started up again in the house. The psychic wanted to know if my son or I had seen any children, and I told her that my son had seen a little girl. The psychic told me that this little girl died either around or inside the house. Since the house is about forty or forty-five years old, the death could have occurred in that time period. The psychic also told me that my husband had left unfinished business here and that is why he keeps coming back. My son and I are upset about the things that happened in the house, given that my husband called the police on my son all the time and the way my husband died. He left an unfinished life, and that is why his soul continues to return. We still hear footsteps and the area downstairs gets extremely cold. I am concerned for my son because when I go to work, he is there alone. I have tried to get him to take some courses through the day program at Chapel Haven, which is a great place for kids with disabilities. They offer a wide variety of courses to take and this really expands their horizons. Chapel Haven is in New Haven, and there is also a branch in Tucson, where he could go if I decide to move there after I retire. My son eventually broke up with his girlfriend Amber and move in with me. He left his apartment that he rented with her. He was now 27 years old.

These hauntings continue, there are less of them in the summer time. They seem to increase as the weather gets colder. I have seen a vortex—a portal between the physical plane and the spiritual plane—in the living room during the winter months, a swirling, funnel shape that I have captured on camera. In the image of the vortex, (image 6) I see three faces—my husband's and those of two other entities.

One afternoon we went to the mall, and I decided to record any sounds in my bedroom while we were gone. I put the digital recorder on the dresser in my room. We left for the mall around 1 p.m. When we came home, I listened to the recorder after dinner. First, there weren't any sounds and then, all of a sudden, there was a bang. It sounded like a door closing. After about a half-hour, there was tremendous static on the recorder. I know that paranormal activity emits electromagnetic charges and assumed that was the reason for the static. I then heard some type of breathing and more banging. I couldn't really tell what was the banging was, but my son said it was the door closing. We did not know who or what this is. My son told me he saw a little girl going up the stairs a few days earlier; and then she disappeared. This little girl had pigtails and was carrying a doll. She asked my son to wind up her doll, and he heard her say, "Mommy, I don't feel well." I told my son that if he saw her again, tell her to go to the light and let me know. My son has also heard my husband's voice downstairs, saying "Where did I put it? Where is it?" This is followed by the sound of cabinets being opened and banging. I don't know what my husband is looking for, but this could be the unfinished business the psychic talked about. Some type of upset happened in this house, maybe even on the day of my husband's death.

Ghosts also appear in a mist. I have included a picture in this book (image 6) showing a face picked up by the video camera. At first, it appeared as a mist alone, and then it was accompanied by other faces. This is another manifestation of paranormal activity in my house.

I am still very upset that I was not at home on the day of my husband's death. I obtained the fire department's report of what happened. It stated that someone called 911 at 5:04 p.m., and the paramedics arrived at the house at 5:11 p.m. It took them seven minutes to arrive, perhaps the door was locked? By the time they arrived, he was dead. I spoke to one of the EMTs, and he told me that my husband had still been warm, but his body had shut down. They tried to revive him numerous times, using CPR and medication for his heart, including atropine and epinephrine, but nothing seemed to work. I know that after three minutes without oxygen, there is brain damage. I read about this in many books. They pronounced him dead at 5:30 p.m. My husband probably did not accept his traumatic death, and he is now an earthbound spirit.

There are times when we hear nothing, as though he has crossed over, but after a few days or so the hauntings start up again: the footsteps on the stairs, the banging, the sounds of moving objects.

I know that the spirits can talk. One night, about two years ago, I came home from the dentist. I wanted to take a nap since I'd had a tooth pulled. I was alone in the house. I opened the door and said to myself, "I feel sick." Then, all of a sudden, I heard my husband downstairs say, "They are saying things about you!" I yelled, "All of you get out!" because I could hear others downstairs as well. My husband never liked anyone to say bad things about me; he would get very mad. He loved me so very much, and he is probably in the house because evil people are trying to give my son and me a hard time. People who are mad about their lives are trying to upset us and make our lives miserable.

The spirits know what is going on. You don't know they are there, but they are. They can listen and see you, but you don't know they are there, listening. This concept is scary, but it's true! I can feel the presence of someone in my room at night, watching me. It might be my husband or some other spirit. All of the sudden, the bedroom gets dark and then light again. This is an ongoing problem that has not been resolved. I would need to hire a bunch of paranormal activity ghost hunters to find out what is really going on. That would be too intrusive for me, and since my son has a handicap, that is not a good idea.

The real question is why do spirits make contact with people. Are they trying to tell us something? Why do my son and me continue to have this torment in our home? There are still questions that must be answered. I think the door for spiritual contact opens when I contact a medium or psychic. The night I was on the phone with the angel-contact medium, an entity appeared in my bedroom. It seems as though the spirits come when a door is opened. I spoke to a priest at my job, and he told me to go to church. But I believe

God does not want us to be involved with the spirit world. As the Scripture states:

> For the living know that they shall die: but the dead know not anything, neither have they any more a reward; for the memory of them is forgotten. Also their love, and their hatred, and their envy, is now perished; neither have they any more a portion forever in anything that is done under the sun. (Ecclesiastes 9:5–6 KJV)

This quote from the Bible tells us that at death there is no memory of your life, but I have seen for myself that the opposite is true. The Bible tells us not to seek contact with the deceased, angels, or saints, not to contact deceased family members or friends. God states there are spiritual dangers lurking for those who attempt to do so. Some people believe these spirits are not their deceased loved ones, but demons.

Why do spirits contact some people and not others. Why have these things happened to my son and me and not to others who have lost loved ones? Perhaps we are more open to spirit contact, even though these spirits may be demonic deceptions and not truly loved ones. It could be God allows this to happen to tell the individuals who are being haunted and harassed by these spirits to go back to the church and be more in tune with God. It is important to turn to God for help in times of trouble. My son and I now go to church every Sunday; we are seeking the help of the Lord. Yet these hauntings still continue.

One morning as I left for work, my son heard someone going up to my bedroom. He heard footsteps on the stairs and then my husband's voice calling for him: "Brad, Brad, I have to tell you something." My son came upstairs, but there was no one there. What was this? Was this my husband coming back from the dead or a demon harassing my son? According to the Bible, it was a demon. Even the good deeds that people credit to the Virgin Mary may be caused by demons. Another quote from the Bible says, "For such are false apostles, deceitful workers, transforming themselves into the apostles of Christ. And no marvel; for Satan himself is transformed into an angel of light" (2 Corinthians 11:13–14 KJV). Sometimes, demons mislead to gain people's trust. Thus, mediums and psychics can enhance demonic activity. I have heard many times how widows see their dead husbands in their bedrooms. They feel their husband's spirit is trying to comfort them. I don't believe that any demonic activities are in my house. I feel that these spirits and angels are trying to help my son and me, that my husband is coming back to see if we are okay.

In the Bible, God clearly tell us that the dead are not able to communicate with us. We cannot communicate with them. God tells us that Satan and other demons are trying to deceive us. What are we to believe? This is a difficult situation for me to consider. I have pictures of what has been going on and continues to happen in my house. Are these angels coming to help us or demonic entities? I believe in my heart and soul that they are good things. This is my husband's spirit watching out for us not any demonic entities. After all, I saved my mother's life once and my husband's life twice. I don't think that any evil would be here in my house.

One night I was watching a TV show called *Hauntings*, and on the show, I saw Rose, the woman who styles my hair. She goes to the homes of people who are experiencing paranormal activity and tries to help them. She belongs to a paranormal society in Connecticut. When she goes to these haunted homes, she takes a bishop from the church and a psychic. I asked her to visit my home on September 18, 2010. I showed her the images that I had recorded on my video camera. She brought some type of meter that would show if there were any type of paranormal activity or energy in the house. We started to talk about the portal, which is where the spirits and other entities enter and leave. I told the woman that I thought the portal was in my bedroom near the window because that is where I saw my husband in shadow form. We went upstairs to my bedroom with the meter, and toward the bottom of the wall near the window, the meter starting going off. Rose asked, "What is downstairs, just underneath your bedroom?" I told her it was my son's bedroom. We went there, and the meter went off toward the wall on the left side of his bed. That is where the portal is. We found the portal! It extends from above my bedroom ceiling near the window straight down to my son's bedroom on the left side.

Rose did not know how to close the portal. In fact, she acted as though it could not be closed. I plan to invite the bishop over to help us with these ongoing problems. My poor son keeps asking me, "Momma, Momma. Why is this still happening?" My answer is, " Honey, you can't control the soul!"

About the Author

Diana Formisano Willett was born in New York City and attended Bernard Baruch College of the City University of New York, where she majored in business administration. She received her degree in 1974. She moved to Connecticut in 1978, when she got married. She now resides in East Haven, Connecticut, and has worked at Yale-New Haven Hospital for the past twenty-eight years.

Notes:

Notes:

Notes:

Notes:

Notes:

Notes:

Notes:

_____

_____

_____

_____

_____

_____

_____

_____

_____

_____

_____

_____

_____

_____

_____

_____

_____

_____

_____

_____

_____

_____

_____

_____

_____

Notes:

_____
_____
_____
_____
_____
_____
_____
_____
_____
_____
_____
_____
_____
_____
_____
_____
_____
_____
_____
_____
_____
_____
_____
_____

Notes:

Notes:

Notes:

_____

_____

_____

_____

_____

_____

_____

_____

_____

_____

_____

_____

_____

_____

_____

_____

_____

_____

_____

_____

_____

_____

_____

_____

_____

_____

_____

Notes:

_____

_____

_____

_____

_____

_____

_____

_____

_____

_____

_____

_____

_____

_____

_____

_____

_____

_____

_____

_____

_____

_____

_____

_____

_____

_____

_____

_____

_____

Notes:

Notes:

Notes:

Notes:

Notes:

Notes: